SURF MUSIC

R. S. DEESE

Pelekinesis

Surf Music by R.S. Deese

ISBN-10: 1938349377
ISBN-13: 978-1-938349-37-9
eISBN: 978-1-938349-58-4
Library of Congress Control Number: 2016953678

Cover artwork:
Aphros by Rupert Deese
Image size: 16 1/4″ × 9 1/2″
Paper size: 27 1/2″ × 19 1/2″
Medium: Drypoint
Paper: Magnani Acquerello, 300 lb. Hot Press
Collaborating Master Printer: Jonathan Higgins

Layout and Book Design by Mark Givens
Author photo by Mariann Murray

First Pelekinesis Printing 2017

For information:
Pelekinesis, 112 Harvard Ave #65, Claremont, CA 91711 USA

◆Pelekinesis
www.pelekinesis.com

SURF MUSIC

poems by
R.S. DEESE

CONTENTS

FOR ISADORA

UNITED STATES

"At the time when radio was in its infancy,
experimentalists midway in the United States
summoned their friends to hear the Atlantic waves and
the Pacific surf simultaneously."
The Glasgow Herald

January 26th, 1924

Sing!
ecstatic intercourse

of the sound of water
channeled with the sound

of water:
surf music

broken sometimes
by the high

& haywire
ringing of the spheres.

Now the shore
is everywhere

and we can hear
a jovial spark

mimic in the circuitry

this resounding

Union,

as it tumbles in the dark.

TWO SNAILS

for R.J.D.

This morning I am half asleep
Water falling everywhere
Pooling in the gutter pipe
Snaking backwards to the shore

Remembering a pair of snails
Yesterday out in the heat
Bonded in their jagged trails
To a ribbon of concrete

On the arid civic skin
Below each brittle, spiral case
A hungry corps of ants flowed in
To scrape away some sustenance

Where these vessels wove a map
Of silver lacing in their wakes
Each filament lit like the crack
Of lightning as it breaks.

HARP

The historian's poor
Durable harp, string off

Center, rusty frame.
Leaves a shape

In the dust.
Hold it. Pluck a while.

Whose harp is this again?
Its only note

Weighs the air
As it falls

And rattles that shattered
Congress of skulls

Near as the brink of the highway.

ROAD RUNNER

Heaven or the promised land
Eternity or soon

Once I spy the vanishing point
I'm out of this cartoon

Meep meep.

TIDE

Really not far
From the beach

But there, beyond the breakers
I thought – even floating – it'd kill me

Clung to my gasp, I hurried
Against it back

Ah, Star Wars towel!
Grateful panting

Slowly in the sand
And safe among

We beaching mass
I saw this suckling make

A tiny fist
To press against his mamma's

Bub
He whimpered like a little man

Afraid of drowning

IF IGNORANCE IS BLISS

If ignorance is bliss,
It's nothing next to this:
The warm, narcotic glow
Of what we think we know.

ESSE QUAM VIDERI

For Curtis Hsiang

I dreamt I saw you this morning, late in a cycle
Of sleep, six years now since you have died.
I was entering some kind of theater or big party

And spoke just seven words to you, before a man
In a dark suit broke in to whisper like a radio:
"Mitt *Romney* is here tonight." In affirmation

I responded: "That's awesome. He's the man."
A lie that made you smile at once, half
Out of pity, half with the malice of a friend.

Why do I buy such time from the living? And why
Do I keep your name and form, embrace them
And say, "Curtis, I am so glad to see you!"

So long since you've moved on to other things?

Watertown, Massachusetts. June 21ˢᵗ, 2006.

THE SCHOLAR OF ALEXANDRIA

He lived in a time when the lights
Were going dim, and every trick of memory
Drew closer to impossible. His nights
Passed in the high hall with the broken
Gates, honoring the sleep of dogs,
And tracing every scratch on stolen
Scrolls of fish paper. By day his back
Was straight again. He was a sure
Magician, his hat soaked in deep black
Ink and crusted with a spew of stars
That split the sun and startled listeners.
He spoke a perfect alchemy of silent
Truths and sonorous inventions. In a day,
He'd pull more coins than he could count;
Spills nine tithes on wine and treats
Then sleep his drunk off like a cat,
To climb back through those sooted gates
And sift more secrets from the trash.

THE YEAR OF THE HORSE

Horses make mistakes
But those mistakes
Are not their own.

Riders make mistakes
But those mistakes
They will not own.

So whose are they?
Neigh! Neigh! Neigh!
So whose are they?
Neigh! Neigh! Neigh!

They belong to the Year of the Horse.

SONG ABOUT TIME & MONEY

When the money is gone
When the time is gone
What you've got is the *what?*
Of what you spent it on,
What you spent it on.

If that *what?* makes you happy
Or sick, or happy and sick,
Just remember this trick:
Try to recall what is *what?*
When you're dead and gone,
Dead and gone.

When the money is gone
When the time is gone
What you've got is the *what?*
Of what you spent it on,
What you spent it on.

SATI

Each of us is widowed
By some light lost to desire

Our burden now is just to know
Not walk into the fire

CHRIST, WHAT DO YOU WANT FROM ME?

He stands at my doorstep

Holding a magazine

With no advertisements

And, of course, it's free.

I can't help but be suspicious.

ENLIGHTENMENT

Clearly, our friend Lucifer
Is working all the switches

Behind any project such as this.
The guy with the flashlight,

The Roman candles, and the
Mental map of all those

Cables, snaking in the dust
Below our feet. Did he

Ever have such awful wings
Under that sorry coat of his?

None of us can remember
Now. He tears his coupons from

The clock and hurries home
With them, too thoroughly beat

After work to be much of a
Nemesis to us. Too certain that

That lottery slip, placed gingerly
Next to his glass of water,

Could crack the lock tomorrow

To resist the shifting

Waves of laughter, light and

Chatter, or tangle his claw

In our blanket of sleep.

THE KINGDOM OF HEAVEN

What better emblem
Could there be
For the inside freedom
Of the heavenly kingdom
Than the lightness I knew
In my gut last week?
I must have squeezed
Three pounds of feces
Clean out of me that morning.
Freed up from my waste
I stepped into the day
With light feet & an undesigned smile.
When asked, "What's new?"
What could I say?

TRUE STORY

I was visiting the zoo
And saw two giant
Tortoises, engaged in

Tortoise intercourse.
I was puzzled
At the age of eight

To see one tortoise
On the other, as
If someone had

Stacked them there.
I tapped the upper
Tortoise, who

(The *moment* that
I touched his shell)
Erupted in ecstasy.

Everyone inside that
Zoo, I thought,
Was laughing at me.

OX MOUNTAIN

A hill above the town where people
go to feed their goats, or else to

gather shrinking scraps of firewood.
So bald, its name is touched

in every crack of local wit
on nervous men or hobbling women

who have lost their hair. Tourists
and classes of children trickle

through here every spring to see
the swept and dusted replica of a

house where Mencius could have lived.
He told stories about Ox Mountain

which he hoped would prove to listeners
that human beings, their thoughts each

one as dry and bitter as a strand
of summer grass that even goats would

skip, were good in their beginnings.
William James (nodding to Hsun Tzu) said

that he was tender-minded. Hawkers
who paint frogs and flowers on butcher

scrolls right on the street, also
paint Ox Mountain pictures, drunk

with the clear blood of a cracked spring,
screaming with bright birds and crickets

who flit through the bent grass and crooked
trees. Fat deer retire in the shade

of ink and water, a small one curling
its shape to sleep between the others.

WHEN THE HEART WILL THIRSTY STRETCH

When the heart will thirsty stretch

Its splitting, feeding web of roots

More into the red mud

On past the lover's face and mother's bub

To drink the cooling blood of springs

And fortify the trunk

So will the mind

With awful stretch of shimmering arms

Annihilate its borders

And receive more of the Sun

ONE DAY IN THE WOODS

Joy rolled up my belly
And down my spine
Like a shot glass of tears
Down a curving blush
While all of named
And unnamed time
Rolled over me
Like water
Down a duck's back

HOW GOD LOVES THE EARTH

God saw the world
and he was hungry for it
so he delighted
in a race of great lizards
to eat it up

And the lizards feasted well
and when their long feasting
had filled up God's belly
they let out his belches
and died making food
for the mud

God was heavy from this
and felt like a nap
so he slept inside
the spotted pelts
of some lazy cats
under a tree

And the cats dreamed dreams
of chasing snacks and fucking
and God liked it
and liked it

R .   S .   D E E S E

until a sucking tick
on his neck
woke him up

He scratched away
the tick and thought
Excellent dreams!
but a billion of them
would still not contain me
I'll make new vessels
for my wants

And so he delighted
in a race of soft apes
whose tender bodies
and spacious minds
dreamed dreams and rhymes
for God to stretch
his limbs inside

SACK OF LIFE

Cheese cloth, dark with oil, across
The wide crotch of a twenty pound
Bird; it never could fly, so we
Stuffed its guts with stalks and grains
And the grounds of fragrances,
Ripped from the stems of wet
Garden flora this very morning.

Our bones are insufficient,
So tools are at the table
This evening: stabbers and cutters
And scooping probes, forged
From a prize in the bowels of
Rocks (across the equator)
To please our eyes,
Dimly, to mind us of the moon.

And porcelain, white as teeth,
In front of every guest; remember,
The whole world was a saucer once, long
Dragons lounging, devouring its edges;
These fled fast the prows of our
Fishers, shattering brine and
Belching like work to compass

All in a close net of names.

Tonight, after dinner, drink,
And the clinking speeches
Of passes and pleases and thanks,
You and I each, overflowing
With wine breath, "I must be going,"
And the slow ache of surfeit
Will wander to straight rivers
To the wide sea, proverbially,

Fumble for the light,
Unfold with lonely dignity,
And cast our shadows.

THE WORK OF ENGINEERS

The vertebrae of sewer pipe
Laid even in a row

The coiled garden hose
Beside the driveway

The train that banks
A mountainside

Above a vale of snow
The shoulder and the breast

Of a new highway

MAGELLAN

What do I know about stars?
Compared to something
I know less about, Eternity,
These are mere fleeting

Sparks cast from a mindless wheel.
I thank God, whom I know
Close to nothing of, that Ferdinand
Magellan was no student of this

Mindless wheel, Eternity, but set his eyes
Upon the fleeting sparks, and whistled
Hymns across a dark Pacific
In his sleeping faith

About their permanence.
They led him in a shimmering
Circle.
A blind embrace.

POOL

Pool tides lap the sweat

Of the suited line swimmers

Who measure each and each

Their wills

To touch and repeat

The opposite walls

Silently chanting the numerals upwards

THE WILD MAN

His spine's become a snake
That's thrilled to be
A man's spine; you can see
Him troubling geese out by the lake

With his hollering howl
That knows no season of the year
No mate who might be anywhere
A heated, apartmental soul

Ejaculates to the wild.

STITCH

If everything
Is new

In Heaven,
Where

Is there
The beauty

Of a thing
That has

Been mended?

THE CLEARING HAND

This feast is a blessing—
meats honeyed and hot
laid wide to our lawn
But God! for the wind
that riles that fence
and blows the smells
of so much feasting
fast away

This wave is a blessing—
that flats where it floods
that spills to my toes
But God! for the pull
drawing it back
back to the broad riot
the sea loves no swamps
at its shores

Whole flesh is a blessing—
to have and to hold
to wrestle and kiss
But God! Thank God!
The whipping sand
cleans bones to gems
and ashes fly as
light as ether

THE OPTIMIST

Seeing a bucket
Half full of shit, he declares
"It is half empty."

405 SOUTH

A bright, tumescent whistle
cuts a path out to the sea

above this ferroconcrete
post, beside this slender tree.

SINK

I remember
the metal tray of watercolors
inside my desk at school.

I never cleaned
my brush, or drained it
well enough, so everything
bled across the palette,
and hardened up like that.
Whenever I had to
fish this out
and open it again,
I felt a pang of shame.

Everywhere,
the primary colors
blinking through
a crusted hurricane:
ninety-percent
earthbound mustard
excrement, the flavors
of a banquet
caught mingling
in a beggar's beard.

Grace

was the steel sink

at the corner

of the room, where I

ran silver water,

a ton of it,

all over that tray,

until the tiny resevoirs

of color

could bleed themselves

into the stream.

I could keep on doing this:

the whole damn thing

as white as bone, water

flowing over it.

NINE SONGS FOR THE
MIRROR & THE MONKEY

I. THE LION'S TOOTH

A subtle foot of curling root
A stalk sewn equal to the breeze
A wreath of Lion's Tooth to cut

The lucky thread of sight that sees
A mirror of the Sun and Moon
Among the grass as tall as trees

This humble flower is the one
The blind of heart still call a weed
One empire cracked and scores begun

By the flight of a single seed

II. THE QUEEN

The dreamer she weaves in her womb
Weaves her into the same dream
Neither knowing who nor whom

Knowing neither be nor seem
Only an illicit thought
That lights creation with its gleam:

One white seed floating from without
Three walls the king built high and strong
To settle in a sweet dark spot

Where it does not belong

III. THE KING

Not quite asleep, the old man muses:
If only I were one with my horse
—A centaur beats a king for most uses—

I'd leave my kingdom (with a force
Of guards to guard it) and taste the air
Outside these walls, then fill my purse

With fat red berries from up there
Where steam breaks from the mountainside
You cannot get such berries here

No thought would break my stride

IV. THE DRAGON

A dragon sleeping in her nest
Draws new iron from old rust
Here she stays to drink her rest

Another eon if she must
Do not wake her to enquire
If her dreams are wise or just

One day, a king drunk with desire
And torn from peace by anger's claw
Will summon her into his fire

As she wraps him in her law

V. THE MONKEY

A man who dreams he is a monkey
Who dreams he is a fish, and a fish
Who dreams she is a dreaming monkey

Who dreams a man but wakes a fish
Are all the same while the fish is awake
And the man still slumbers in his wish

What difference, really, does it make
Who is a fish, a monkey, or a man?
None but this: The world will break

To wake the sleeping man

VI. THE ASSASSIN & THE SECRETARY

Every kingdom since the first

That brought the wild to order

From the finest to the worst

Folds lies into its charter

And spills the blood of innocents

As lime into its mortar

To bind great stones into a fence

A king must guard the art of killing

And gather jewels of high expense

As honors for the willing

VII. TAHUALAMNE

You will never remember how to spell
Her name, or the way her face
Shines in the dusk, or even tell

If what lingers in your eye's a trace
Of something real, or just a thing
You hoped and hope for. The place

And time are sunk in the flood. Nothing
Happened you can be sure. The one
Who taught your bow at once to sing

That one is gone

VIII. THE PRIEST

Important lies ought never go
Out poor & naked. They must glisten
In the half light with the glow

Of miracles. Every ear will listen
To the music of a lie well told
As every eye will fasten

On the bird whose wings are trimmed with gold.
And simple folk must never sing (except to sing *along*)
Their minds should never be as bold

As their bones are strong

IX. THE GRATEFUL BABOONS

We wandered over scorching flats
Through mazes thickly twined
We fled from ravenous snakes and cats

But no shelter could we find
Until an arrow from above
Saved the smallest of our kind

It echoed in the shady grove
Where on that day we came to roam
Whistling a song of love

We prayed would lead us home
Whistling a song of love
We prayed would lead us home

THE STAIRS

Was what I said clever?
Did it cleave?

I can't remember. I
am descending, naked as

a naked man, down flatly
bent concrete of stairs.

They sweat, and coldly
kiss my feet.

I mumble through my ears.

TALK ABOUT THE WEATHER

It is that safe, familiar brand of speech
That bores us right away, but fills the hollow
Intervals through which it tends to blow
Occasioning a "Yes, I know!" from persons each
A stranger or acquaintance to the other
As they wait in line, or anyplace
Where we must navigate a funnel, face
To face. Another space where talk of weather
Whistles welcomely to ward off silence
Is through that steep and staggering crevasse
That suddenly or glacially may pass
Between the touch and tongues of ones once
Intimate, who now share only civil chatter
On the life of air, and fire, and water.

KITE SEASON

Line as bright
as powdered bleach

and nearly thin
enough to cut

your fingers,
taut between

the anchor
of your body

and the currents
in the sky.

The kites themselves
like all the toys

the supermarket sells:
eagerly disposable,

except the fragile
skin of these

was not part
of some luring lie,

but parcel
of their buoyancy.

PEN

How quietly you wrote yourself
on the table of my heart;

what was the instrument, the ink,
and how could you,

with so few wiles, sneak them
past my sight?

I think it was a blade of grass,
as weak as anything,

but brave enough to bend
itself against my weight, to touch

its point against a point, back of
my naked neck.

My eyes were closed
that afternoon, against the power

of the sun, as you inscribed
each brilliant point

and then one more,
and then one more, until I saw

the open sky
inside the grateful shadow of my skull.

ROUTE 33

Cuyama wets her bed.

Even when her bed is dry, she shows you
the shape of water. She pulled a big white Cadillac

into the sack and baptized a new member of the Cuyama
yacht club. She swept a black angus away,

she was so hungry once. All the rocks study or speak is water:
Even when the wind is dry, they compare the wind to water.

The footprint of a bobcat bakes into her silt
and sun-swept bed, beside the roots

of a well-traveled tree; it will last much longer
than the footprint of a bobcat in the sand.

LEAVING THE MOVIES

Now, the drama of the parking lot:
the temper of the afternoon reflected

on a spacious screen of blacktop.
A few cars negotiate the spaces

and the common space.
Others wait for the return

of spectators, whose faces
will tighten at the prospect of the sun,

one generous catastrophe.
An engine sputters once and starts to run.

EASTER SUNDAY

Today, I contemplate the cats who
lounge on the back porch
of my parents' house in Claremont,
California.
They come here twice a day to collect
what's offered

in the way of dry cat food, and
sometimes table scraps,
but they will never let a person near
enough to touch them.
As I gaze at seven cats, through the
plate glass sliding door

which is, in this relation, a
shimmering wall of feline fear,
I believe I love them. Maybe since the
memory of touching other cats
still lingers in the gap between us, or
maybe my love is mere

admiration for the color of their eyes,
the canoe-shape of their pupils,

the way they groom themselves, their
arcane allegiances
and swift insouciance. I am not a cat
and nothing in my being,

no instinct or necessity, requires me to
be with them, and yet
I feel this way. If I were not a human
being, but a cat like them,
a figure in their drama, their cruel
and languid history

of mealtimes and quarrels, it would be
a miracle beyond the scope
of mere belief if my love for each of
them could still remain
as perfect as it seems today, behind
this flawless plate glass wall,

above this honeyed cup of tea, that
radiates its warmth into my palms.

AL JEBR

Spine,
great highway

from clitoris
to brain:

from sense
to touch

and back
again;

who can
divide

this sentence?

DRIVE

On this birthday,
I expect to find

my oracle
much closer now

somewhere on
the surface

of my skin.
I drive a car

through Monument
Valley. Seashells

of bottles glitter
everywhere

and glitter again.

ONLY NORTH

Whenever an idiot
Speaks the truth

It burns the paint
Off of my compass.

THE BEACH, CA. 1969

for Helen Deese

The world was never safe.
Each wave ahead was always
Green and menacing
And full of life.
Unlike a person or an angry dog,

A wave won't speak its threats
Beforehand. It just throws you down,
Roars
Its bright, diminished triumph
And falls back into the sea.

As old as all the fingers
On my hand, I could dig for sand crabs
With a blue translucent plastic
Cup. Or just look.
The world was, and is, fantastic.

You knew that, and you know it.
You held all my years that day
And taught me
How to leap above some broken waves
And dive beneath the rise of others.

TOP

seed!

stout pinnacle of

of water, light and minerals:

conspiracy

the slow

a weed,

of

The momentum

PERFECT FAITH

She broke the fruit apart
and offered it to him.

Without a word,
he broke her neck

and made the serpent
tremble on the limb.

"Who will you love?"
God whispered

through a veil of stars,
above his devoted son

and his pale companion.
"No one but you," said Adam.

ECLIPSE

I'm standing due south
of the State House,

watching my collective shadow
pass across the moon.

Above this weave
of civic lights,

I see what's been diminished
as slowly as the minute

hand, as slowly as
the minute hand return.

A tunnel built for passengers,
my line back to the suburbs

is humming through the grass
below my feet.

Boston, Passover 1996.

CITIZEN

Fat torso in a tight gray double-breasted suit
Iridescent necktie made of feathers

He navigates the colored trash and newspapers
Beside my feet on thin, red-stockinged legs

Methodically alert, he reads the smell
Of nourishment somewhere inside the wrappers

His talons grip a golden sheet as he tears into it
The crescent of a cheeseburger, far too big

To eat at once, he guards it from the others

BULLETIN

for R.J.D.

Our emblems of merit,
All overboard.

Their perfect gravity
Draws them

To the bottom of the sea.
They will speak

To the rare beam of light
That meets the ocean floor

From time to time,
Or not.

Follow them, and drown.
Remember them

And be checked at every step
By a force no one can see.

Forget them, if you can
Imagine that forgetting sets us free.

Above remain what common gems
May guide a sailor's course

Across the sea.

SIGNATURE

Each time that I'm most legally myself,
I ride these windblown loops & jump

These broken rails: my Sincerity,
My Consent, my Solvency or Insolvency.

Again, the same weak thrill of doubt
And buried fantasy hovers at my elbow:

Do I look cramped? Do I look insane?
Could I do this on the skin of a baseball?

AVOID THE COMPANY OF POETS

Avoid the company of poets
Their poems did not come from them

They shovel food into their throats
& choke up strands of knotty phlegm

Before they slip into their coats
And head back out again.

Their poems did not come from them
Avoid the company of poets

ETERNITY WILL NOT CONFESS

Eternity will not confess
The debt of time to consciousness

But shifts the burden of the rhyme
Demanding consciousness serve time.

TABULA RASA

If I could explain this universe
With a ballpoint pen

It wouldn't be in one spiral notebook
Or ten billion, college ruled

But on your skin after school
In the cool light of your parents' house

While they are off on the business of working or dying
Or whatever it is they do.

I would draw each star and planet
Each ripple of each nebula

Each feather of each comet's tail
On the rise and fall of your belly, the small of your back

And up your spine to the quiet place
Behind your waterfall of hair;

I would draw the nearest stone on the most precise
Of all your toes, and the farthest sun

At that point on your earlobe where we both know
It shines, light enough to tickle

But always hard enough to leave a mark.
Our map would be perfect, true and complete

Though we won't say how or why.
Our secrets still unknown to us,

We do not think to ask.

ARBOR DAY

I was born a lemur
Among the tribe of birds

Navigating through their song
Foraging for words.

HIS ORIGINAL POSSESSION

For Rick Noble

He gave up a plane
Loaded with weapons
For one with none

He gave up a plane
With powerful engines
For one with none

He gave up a pair
Of brilliant wings
Wider than a house

For what whose span
We cannot reckon
But can recall:

His original possession.

DESIGN DEPARTMENT

Goodbye, gumball rocket fin!
Goodbye, bonehead dreams of flight!

The angry box has lumbered in.
Goodbye, flirtatious tail light!

THIS BLUE ELEVENTH MONTH

This blue eleventh month
Finds the topmost leaf

Right at the brink
Of dust

Long Roman ducts
Bear drinks to no one

(their stones are cherished still)
So with this leaf

Its webbing bones
A strip design

Of drinking genius

POSTHUMOUS FAME

Tyrannosaurus Rex, I've read
Is the most popular

Dinosaur, with *Velociraptor*
Gaining since Jurassic Park

Became a major franchise.
Being popular means something

To almost everyone, and T. Rex
Looks like the sort

Who might care more than most
About its name and reputation.

That's why it's kind of sad to think
Of how a predator like T. Rex

Was, without a doubt, despised
By other dinosaurs, and probably

Lacked the foresight to guess
That its stunted arms & deadly grin

Would be everywhere today.

YOUR FONDEST DREAMS

Your fondest dreams
Have all been realized

And already lie in ruins
To the eye of one

Who lives forever
So, although you wouldn't

Guess it, it could be kind
Of lucky that you don't.

REMEMBERING MY DREAMS

Piecing together
A coffee-stained map

I tore apart in anger
In the rain.

After a while,
I'll admit I'm lost

& settle down to sleep again.

SAW

What a fool I was
To hide

My errors.
The serrated

Zigzag
Of my misguided

Path
Is an unwieldy

Saw, it's true
But a saw

That cuts.

SHELTER

The voice
Of a remembered

Friend will open
Sometimes

Like an aural
Umbrella

As the voices
Of the living

Fall like rain.

PATIENCE

The haste-eaten mind
Calls patience a virtue
(A frayed tightrope
'twixt hope & hope)
And keeps on cursing time.

Patience is no more a virtue
Than the ocean is.
The ocean bears all ships
Is cut by every keel
And mercilessly

Forgets them all.

SONG FOR MY CAT

Hear ye! Hear ye!
Hear ye, kitty cat!

I intend with this pen
To scribe you a 'scription

Concerning one thread
That speeds through creation

That winds our cat's cradle
Fingers and all, so let it

Run on through your ears
As taut as any harp string

And listen for a little
While I pluck:

From the thirstiest roots
To the heaviest fruits

From the eye of the lover
To the eyes of the other

It fires its living tangle
In and about the rocks and the corpses

From the fiddler's hand
To the seed's metamorphosis

It speeds like Silly
String springs free

Out of the can
Or, like a knot too tight

May utterly destroy a man
So know ye, little kitty cat

That this strand
From which you're sewn

Is the same
Which will unravel you

That the necklace
And the noose

Are each just portions of its length
As the engine and caboose

By joints enjoy
A single strength

And that stranger, lover, friend and foe
Although they may seem otherly

And though it just cannot
Seem so

Are that same thread as thee.

FORECAST

Late snow
Betrayed by rain

On the third
To last day

Of December.
What we hope

& what we get,
Each a weight

On the scale
Of our senses.

IN DIVERS KINDS OF TONGUES

Quoth
The mystic:

Unplug the radio
By your bed

To tune the radio
In your head

Or, good luck playing
Both.

IN THE CAPITAL

In the capital
The plazas are paved

With quartz,
And the reflecting

Pool's alive with fish
Swum down

From the mountains
To navigate

This rectilinear
Network

Of channels & bays.
Citizens fish in the shade

Of the hall where we
Deliberate

All day, and think nothing of it.

LIFE IS A CONJUGAL VISIT

Every mind
Is a note

In a musical net
That unwinds

On one end
& composes

Itself
On the other.

If this tune
Had a name

I suppose
It could be:

"Life is a Conjugal Visit"

LIGHTS

If you wake up
With a movie

Theme song stuck
Inside your head

It could be a good sign.
You, too

Could be a hero.

MALHEUR

A donut's not
If there's no

Hole in it,
And civil rights

Are not
If there's no

Space
Inside the law

Where air & earth
& sun & sea

Find charter
As the property

Of none.

MINNOW

More nimble than a lumbering
Tradition, a single thought

Darts the thicket
Of speech & memory

From living tongue to ear
To tongue

& from remembered
Tongues to living

Tongues
Or, as a careful thread

Of stains, from the long
Unspeaking dead

To a number of the mute unborn.

MUSIC OF THE WOMB

for Mary Cory

Before they are born
A litter of cubs

Must hear
Their mother's

Heartbeat.
Every season

They will know
Is in

That sound.

A NEW PAIR OF BOOTS

A new pair of boots
Embrace my feet

Like two felicitous
Bear traps

Or two dutiful
Immigrant brides

To a pair
Of homely brothers.

RED

for Hart Deese

The bridge that hangs a circle's sweep
To the tangent of the street
And holds our passage up between its cords

Crosses air & earth & sea
With a spare integrity
Lighter than a spoken chain of words

CROSSING

A poet must be
A pedestrian

Even on a rocket
To the moon.

DO YOU MIND?

Doctor's shrinking
Chalk clacked & scrawled

The board:
Should the mind

Be chaste
And chastened?

Or should it be
Somnambulant

And hastened
By the pull

Of one & one
Thousand

Senses?
Let the question

Rest, for now.
It will be

All of these.

NOT EVEN THE STARS ARE SAFE

A vehicle of glass and steel
Bears us to the top
Of Cadillac Mountain.
The substance and shape
Of car and peak
Both forged by fire
Once recently, once long
Ago, both scraped up
From underneath
An order of shapes
That dignified a moment
Then wandered off as clouds.

Minerals forged by fire seem
Most permanent to us,
But the divisions of trees
On this igneous
Rock speak the power
Of something else, forgetting
And repeating, forgetting
And repeating,
Wearing away hard work of fire.

Not even the stars are safe.

RELIGION, I GUESS

Religion, I guess, is a marvelous town
Of temples, schools & secret retreats

On the floor of a silent sea.
If you could hold your breath for long enough

To swim its boulevards and alleys
And spy its sacred places, you might find

As others have, a reason to believe.

THE ROPES

Just as your life
Is larger than you

So is your tally
Of grace

And reckoning.
It's best to see

Each slip of slack
As nothing but a gift

And each painful
Ratcheting

As yet another
Slip of slack

Slipping
Somewhere else.

Not a soul
Can guess the hand

That draws & releases us.

SPINOZA'S APPRENTICE

Three points
A triangle

Four triangles
A tetrahedron

Yet I still trip
On disbelief

That crystals
Need no help

To make themselves.

MOON ROCK IN THE CUPBOARD

There's a moon rock in the cupboard
Sitting on the middle shelf
When the cupboard door's cracked open
It's a moon unto itself

Spreading moonlight on the dishes
Spreading moonlight on mugs
From the lamplight in the kitchen
It makes moonlight for the bugs

Now, the bugs have clever Witches
And the bugs have solemn Priests
And from the crusts that they can find
They have their Full Moon Feasts

But the Priests see their apocalypse
And the Witches from their powers are cut
When a careful person takes a dish
And leaves the cupboard tightly shut.

THAT WORD

That word is a stone
megaphone
my arms are too weak
to pick up today.
I'll just take my pencil
and be on my way.

LULLABY

Little bird, I know
How your mind darts

Through its net
Of tiny rivers

What you know
Now's what you

Know in your blood
Your heart is a solemn

Emergency
That hums its purple

Rhythm
Through the eggshell

Of your crown
The sun is too much

So you nestle
Here

The wind is too much
So you nestle

Here
A memory

Or premonition,
It's all the same

To me:
The shadow

Of your mother
Is the first place

That you ever were.

SURF MUSIC

I woke up in Fresno
and heard the sound

of Highway 99:
a tunnel of white noise

bisecting the pink
morning light

of the Central Valley.
It was a kind of surf music:

less the sound
of engines running

than the sound of air,
embracing and releasing

something on its way
to somewhere.

This evening,
I am resting on a glacial

slab of granite
somewhere in Kings

Canyon, beside a waterfall.
Minus the combustion,

and the mute complexity
of so much human

freight, the rush
I hear tonight

is the same sound.

R . S . DEESE

ACKNOWLEDGMENTS

In 2000, Manneken Press published the very first *Surf Music*, which included nine of my poems alongside nine original monochrome prints by my brother, Rupert Deese. Creating that chapbook was an incredible experience and it began the journey that led to this volume. I am deeply indebted to my brother Rupert for his powerful and undulating images, then and now, and to Jonathan Higgins of Manneken Press for the extraordinary craftsmanship that he brought to that collection. Mark Givens, the founder of Pelekinesis, has brought an equally exemplary level of skill and professionalism to the production and completion of this book.

I must also thank the following journals for first publishing some of the poems that now appear here: *AGNI* ("Eclipse"), *Berkeley Poetry Review* ("How God Loves the Earth"), *MungBeing* ("Song About Time & Money," "Arbor Day," "Design Department," "Citizen," "Tabula Rasa," "The Queen," and "The Kingdom of Heaven"), *The New Formalist* ("The Lion's Tooth"), *Poetry Motel* ("The Scholar of

Alexandria"), *Poetry Pacific* ("Road Runner"), Gordon Lish's *The Quarterly* ("The Stairs"), and *Whispering Campaign* ("Only North").

Thanks are due to the various venues that hosted readings of the poems in this book, including the Boston Playwrights Theatre at Boston University, the Toby Moss Gallery in Los Angeles, the Nancy Hoffman Gallery in Manhattan, Spoonbill & Sugartown Booksellers in Brooklyn, and the Chinati Foundation in Marfa, Texas.

It would be impossible to thank all of the great teachers I have been lucky to know over the years, but I would like to express my gratitude here for those high school teachers who inspired me and guided me just as I was beginning to write: Rosemary Adam, Jack Knapp, Jim Hill, and Marilyn Penn. I would also like to thank Rosanna Warren for her exacting notes on several of these poems. Even the ones I did not change are the better for it. On a personal note, I must give thanks for the love and support of my late parents, Rupert Julian Deese and Helen Deese, and for the home full of books, music, movies, plays, conversation, and writing that they created for their children. In my memory, battered as it is by age and experience, I can still hear and feel the electric typewriter they gave me during my freshman year of high school. It would be nice to claim that I was destined to write poems, but if I subtract the immediate and visceral pleasures that little typewriter gave me, with its hum and the striking sound of its hammers, it becomes harder to imagine how I would have begun.

In closing, I offer my humble gratitude to my wife, Isadora Deese, for her love, inspiration, and support. This book is for her.

ABOUT THE AUTHOR

R.S. Deese grew up in Claremont, California. He currently teaches History at Boston University and is the author of *We Are Amphibians: Julian and Aldous Huxley on the Future of Our Species* (University of California Press, 2014). His poetry has been published in *AGNI*, *Berkeley Poetry Review*, *MungBeing*, *The New Formalist*, *Poetry Motel*, and *The Quarterly*.